Donated with funds from
Neva Lomason Memorial Library
Penny Box
through the Friends of the Library
Matching Gift Program, 2007

 W9-ALN-167

DISCARD

WEST GA REG LIB SYS
Neva Lomason
Memorial Library

KRONG!

by Garry Parsons

tiger tales

For Patricia

Jake and his dog, Ace, were playing in the backyard when a spaceship landed. Out stepped an alien and an alien dog.

"Hello!"

said Jake.

"Woof!"

said Ace.

"Krong!"

said the alien.

"Zoff!"

said the alien dog.

Jake ran into the house to get his mom.

"Mom!" Jake called. "There's someone in the yard who doesn't speak any English and he has a dog."

"Maybe he speaks French," said Jake's mom.

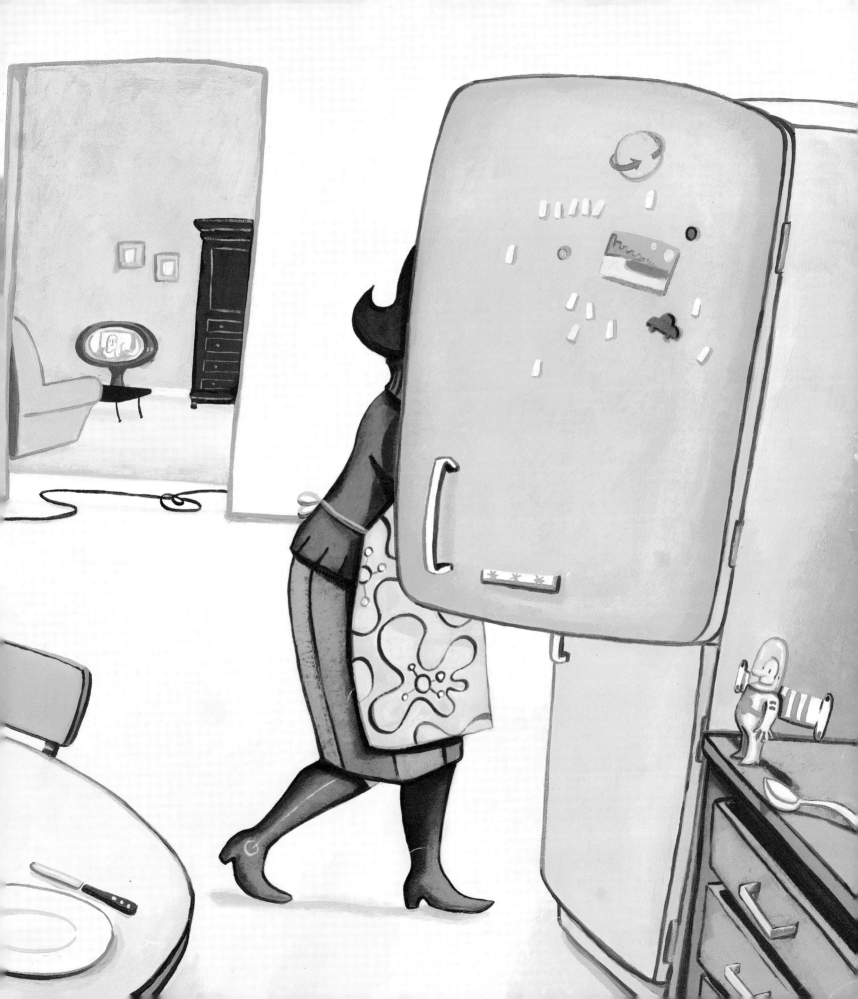

Jake ran back into the yard.

"Chabba

"Zoff,"
said the
alien dog.

chooba!"

said the alien.

"Dad!" Jake called. "There's someone in the yard who doesn't speak any English or French and he's got a dog."

"Maybe he
speaks Spanish,"
said Jake's dad.

Jake ran back into the yard.

"Hola!"

said Jake.

That's "hello" in Spanish.

"Guau guau,"

said Ace.

"Mom! Dad!" Jake called. "The person in the yard doesn't speak any English or French or Spanish, and neither does his dog."

"Maybe he speaks Japanese,"
said Jake's mom and dad.

Jake ran back into the yard.

"Konnichiwa!"
said Jake.

"Wan wan,"
said Ace.

That's "hello" in Japanese.

"Zabba zooba zemer Zoo!" said the alien.

"Zoff," said the alien dog.

"Jabba jooba noo poo loo!"

said the alien, holding out a present.

"Mom! Dad!"
Jake called.

"The person in the yard
doesn't speak any English or
French or Spanish or Japanese,
and neither does his dog, but he
has a present and it

might
be
for
me!"

"Does he have one eye, yellow skin, four fingers, and a spaceship?" asked Jake's dad.

"Yes," said Jake.

"And a dog that only says 'zoff'?" said Jake's mom.

"That's right," said Jake.

"Then that would be your Uncle Phil from the planet Noo," said Dad.

"He's come to visit," said Mom, "and he speaks...
Noobanese!"

Jake raced back outside.

"Kro

"Kr

"Zoff!"

said Uncle
Phil's dog.

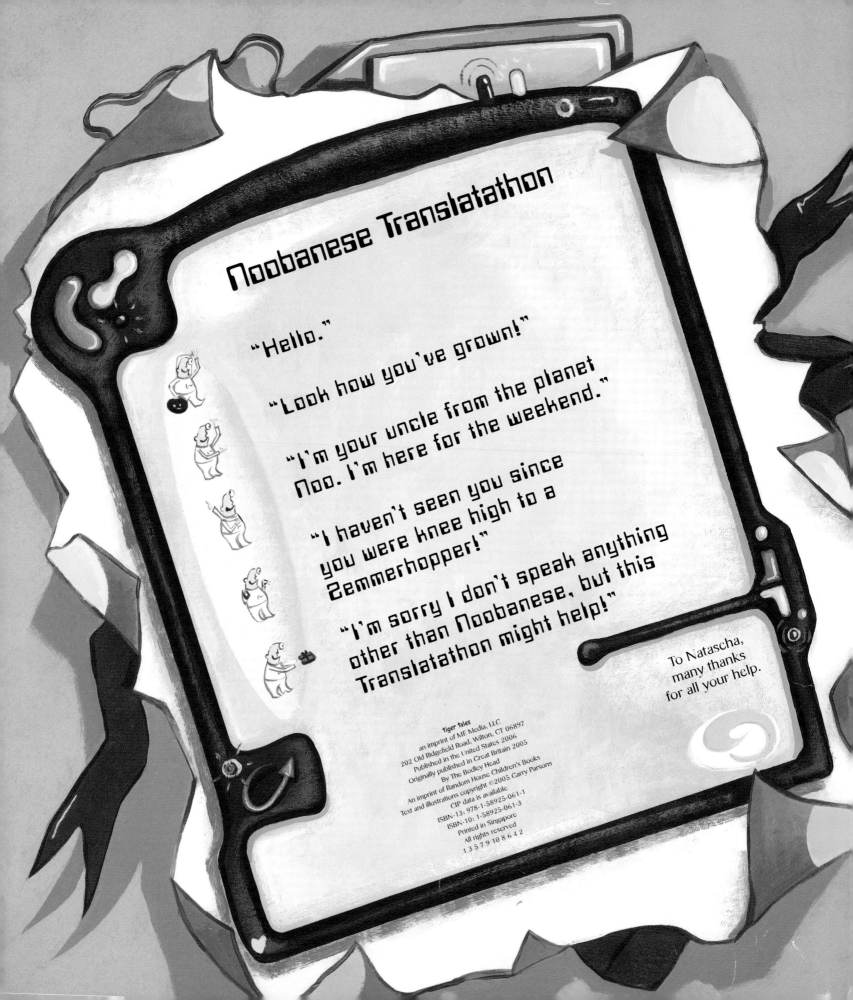

Noobanese Translatathon

"Hello."

"Look how you've grown!"

"I'm your uncle from the planet Noo. I'm here for the weekend."

"I haven't seen you since you were knee high to a Zemmerhopper!"

"I'm sorry I don't speak anything other than Noobanese, but this Translatathon might help!"

To Natascha,
many thanks
for all your help.

tiger tales
an imprint of ME Media, LLC.
202 Old Ridgefield Road, Wilton, CT 06897
Published in the United States 2006
Originally published in Great Britain 2005
By The Bodley Head
An imprint of Random House Children's Books
Text and illustrations copyright ©2005 Garry Parsons
CIP data is available
ISBN-13: 978-1-58925-061-1
ISBN-10: 1-58925-061-3
Printed in Singapore
All rights reserved
1 3 5 7 9 10 8 6 4 2

Krong! /
E PARSO   **31057010267261**
Parsons, Garry.
WEST GA REGIONAL LIBRARY SYS